Francis Poulenc

Sonata
for clarinet and piano

Revised edition, 2006

Edited by Millan Sachania

Includes audio demonstration and accompaniment tracks

Consulting editor: Patricia Harper (1994)
with historical introduction and editorial commentary in English, French and German.

This piece has been arranged for flute and orchestra by Lennox Berkeley;
score and parts are available on hire from the publisher.

CH83556

ISBN 978-1-78305-951-5

Edited and supervised by Sam Lung.
Clarinet recorded by Joy Farrall.
Piano recorded by Huw Watkins.
Audio mixed and mastered by Imogen Hall and Jonas Persson.
With special thanks to Dom Kelly and the English Session Orchestra.

Exclusive Distributors:
Hal Leonard
7777 West Bluemound Road
Milwaukee, WI 53213
Email: info@halleonard.com

Hal Leonard Europe Limited
42 Wigmore Street
Marylebone, London, W1U 2RY
Email: info@halleonardeurope.com

Hal Leonard Australia Pty. Ltd.
4 Lentara Court
Cheltenham, Victoria, 3192 Australia
Email: info@halleonard.com.au

To acces audio visit:
www.halleonardmgb.com/mylibrary

1528-5803-5740-4354

Chester Music

Francis Poulenc

SONATA FOR CLARINET AND PIANO

Poulenc completed the Sonata for Clarinet and Piano at Brive-Noizay late in the summer of 1962. The project had been occupying his thoughts for at least five years. He had drafted the slow movement as early as August 1959, but the demands of the *Gloria*, then in the final stages of composition, halted further progress. It was under these circumstances that Poulenc noted to R. Douglas Gibson of J. & W. Chester that the slow movement could be published as an independent 'Andantino tristamente', were he never to complete the outer movements. (The 'Andantino' later donated its 'tristamente' label to the first movement, and in the process acquired the title 'Romanza'.) Poulenc's perseverance won through, however, and in a letter dated 18 January 1963 the composer promised Gibson delivery of the fair copy within eight days. He also requested that the task of engraving the work be entrusted to 'un bon graveur assez musicien pour deviner les notes douteuses'. Twelve days later, Poulenc suddenly died. The notational ambiguities thus remained unresolved and accordingly contaminated the text of the first edition, which was published later that year.

The revised edition of 1973, prepared with the assistance of Thea King and Georgina Dobree, attempted to grapple with these textual problems. But though it made a number of useful suggestions, the scope of its amendments did not extend to improving the rough-and-ready notational style of its predecessor. In addition, a number of significant inaccuracies escaped detection.

In preparing the present edition, the direct successor to that of 1973, I have taken the opportunity to re-inspect Poulenc's fair copy. My objectives have been to reassess Poulenc's intentions, to remedy patent errors in the 1973 edition, and, wherever possible, to refine and clarify the notation. The underlying aim has been to construct a score for performing musicians along scholarly lines.

My treatment of Poulenc's accidentals has been much guided by the necessity of providing a precise but legible score. Thus the new edition encloses within square brackets accidentals that were plausibly intended by Poulenc but which are absent from the manuscript. By contrast, accidentals that are almost certainly omitted from the manuscript in error are inserted tacitly. In seeking legibility, the score both provides many cautionary accidentals not present in either Poulenc's fair copy or the 1973 text and excises Poulenc's many redundant accidentals.

The current edition also occasionally redistributes notes between the piano staves in order to enhance its visual appeal. But in this matter, as with all notational issues in the present score, the configuration is undisturbed where Poulenc's notation might have performance or other musical implications.

Perhaps the most immediately noticeable difference between the present edition and its predecessor is in the way in which they slur phrases that conclude with tied notes. The 1973 score follows Poulenc in generally ending the slur on the first of the tied notes, excluding the subsequent note or notes from the phrased unit. By contrast, the present edition consistently extends such slurs so that they incorporate the second or final tied note.

With respect to dynamic and articulation markings, parallel passages in Poulenc's manuscript do not necessarily enjoy identical levels of detail. The new edition refrains from automatically imposing consistency between such passages. In a few instances where the omission of such markings in a second or later statement of a passage is patently erroneous, it rectifies the situation tacitly. 'Corrections' more open to debate, however, appear within square brackets.

A final point: the previous edition gave certain editorial suggestions which suppressed Poulenc's own dynamic markings. The new edition restores the original indications but retains (within square brackets) some of the proposals made by its predecessor for balancing the dynamic levels of the two instruments.

MILLAN SACHANIA
Shepperton, England, 2000

Note on the 2006 edition

In preparing the 2006 edition, I have taken the opportunity to enhance the graphic presentation of the score, clarify some slurs and ties, and put right a couple of minor misprints. There are no major departures, however, from the 2000 edition.

M.S

SONATA

for Clarinet in Bb and Piano

FRANCIS POULENC

I

Allegro tristamente

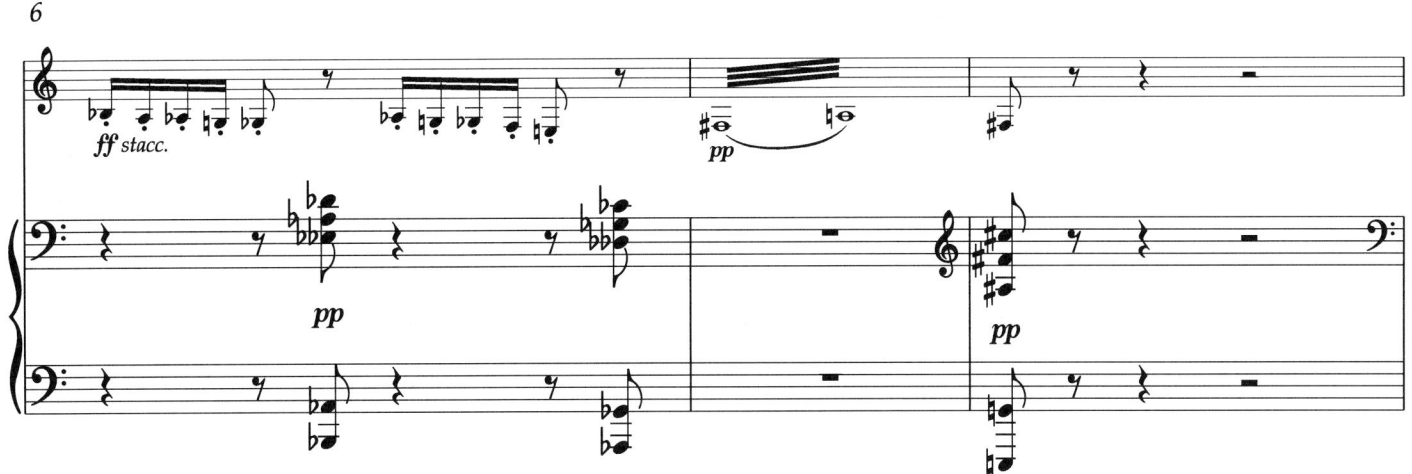

8

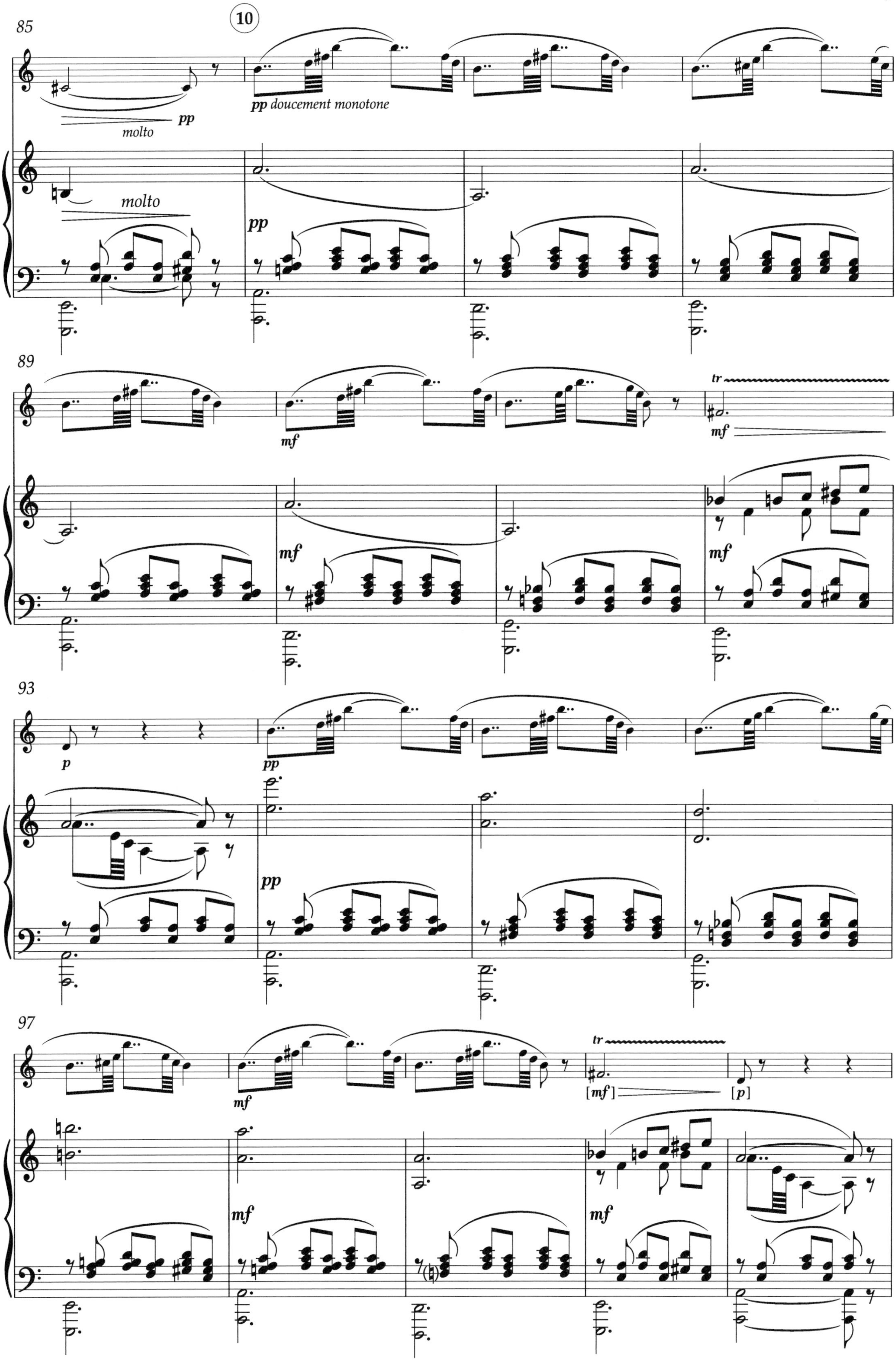
85
10
pp doucement monotone
molto
pp
molto
pp
89
tr
mf
mf
mf
mf
mf
93
p
pp
pp
97
tr
mf
[mf]
[p]
mf
mf

II
Romanza

effleurer (beaucoup de pédale)

III
Allegro con fuoco

mettre beaucoup de pédale

Eté, 1962

Francis Poulenc

Sonata
for clarinet and piano

Revised edition, 2006

Edited by Millan Sachania

Includes audio demonstration and accompaniment tracks

Clarinet part

Chester Music

SONATA

for Clarinet in B♭ and Piano

FRANCIS POULENC

I

Allegro tristamente

4

II
Romanza

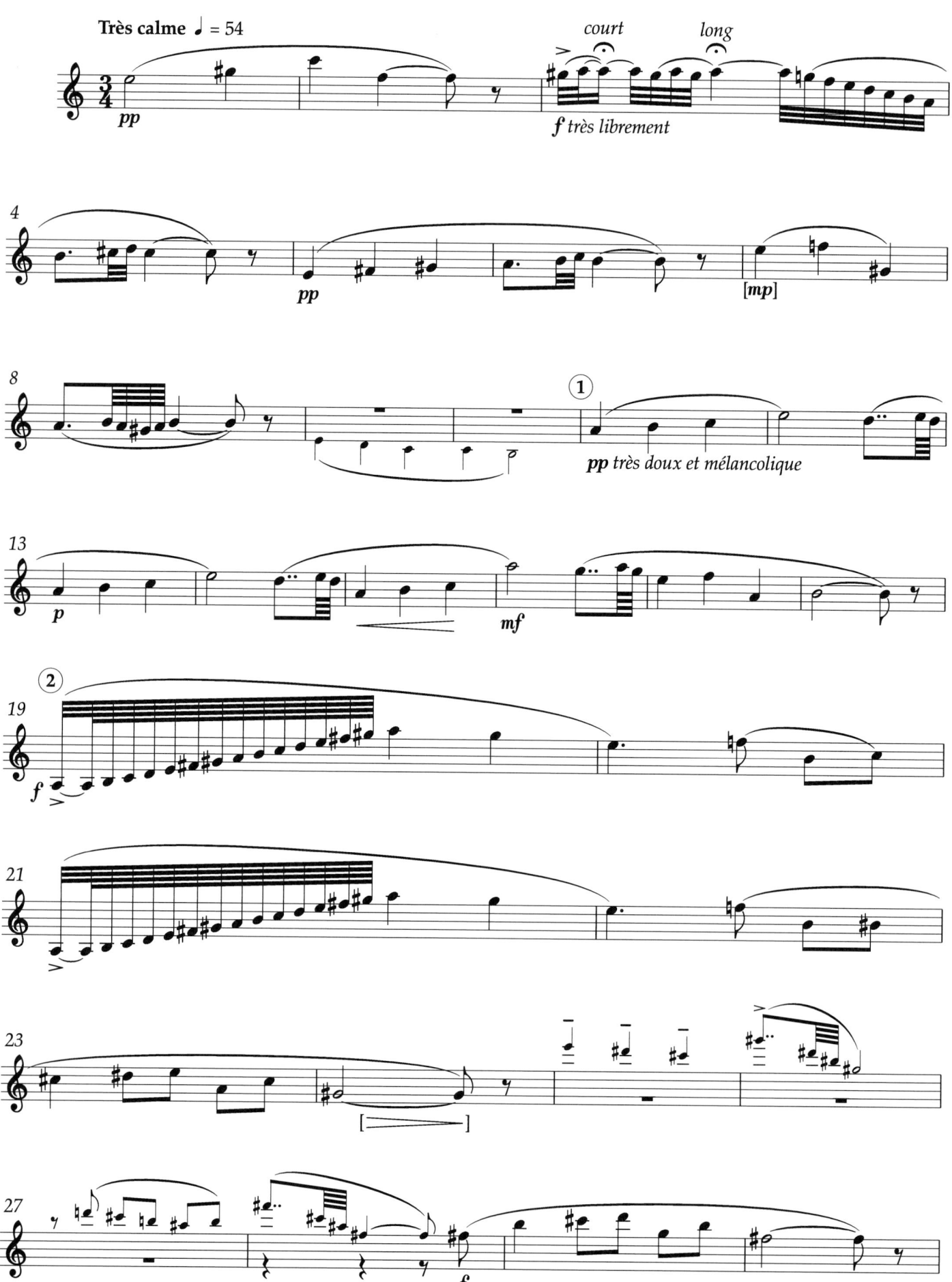

8

III
Allegro con fuoco

Eté, 1962

Selected works by
Francis Poulenc

1899–1963

Piano Solo
Album of Six Pieces
    Mouvements perpétuels No. 1
    Presto from Suite in C
    Impromptu No. 3
    Française
    Novelette No. 1
    Promenade No. 1 (A Pied)
Five Impromptus
Mouvements perpétuels
Three Novelettes
    No. 1 in C major
    No. 2 in B♭ minor
    No. 3 in E minor (on a theme of Manuel de Falla)
Ten Promenades
Suite in C

Piano Duet
Sonata (Prelude–Rustique–Final)
    (also suitable for two pianos, four hands)

Chamber Music
Elégie for horn and piano
Mouvements perpétuels
    orchestrated by the composer for 9 players (1946)
    arr. Heifetz, violin and piano
    arr. Levering, flute and guitar
    arr. Levering, 2 guitars
Sextet for piano, flute, oboe, clarinet, horn and bassoon
Sonata for flute and piano
Sonata for oboe and piano
Sonata for clarinet and piano
Sonata for two clarinets
Sonata for clarinet and bassoon
Sonata for horn, trumpet and trombone
    (also transcribed Nestor for flute and guitar)
Trio for oboe, bassoon and piano
Rapsodie nègre for low voice and two violins, viola,
    cello, flute, clarinet in B♭ and piano

Chester Music

EXCLUSIVELY DISTRIBUTED BY

HAL•LEONARD®

Order No. CH83556